Making Friends

Sheila Hollins and Terry Roth
Illustrated by Beth Webb

Beyond Words

London

D1437981

46 808 664 4

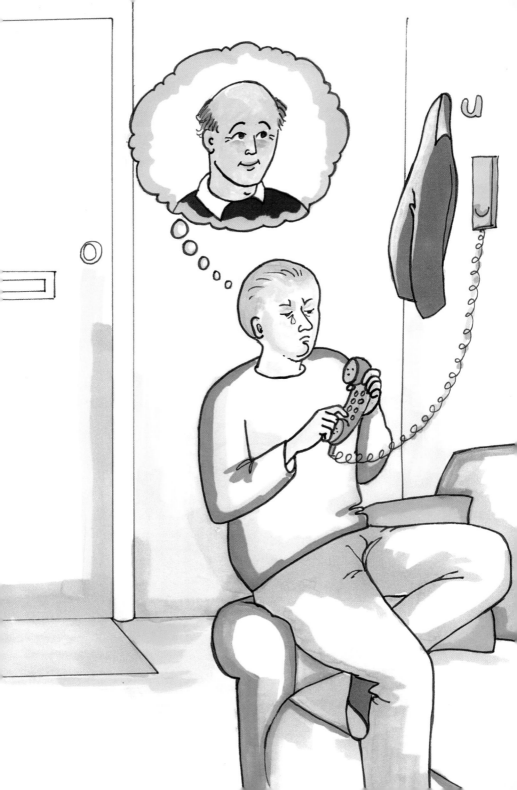

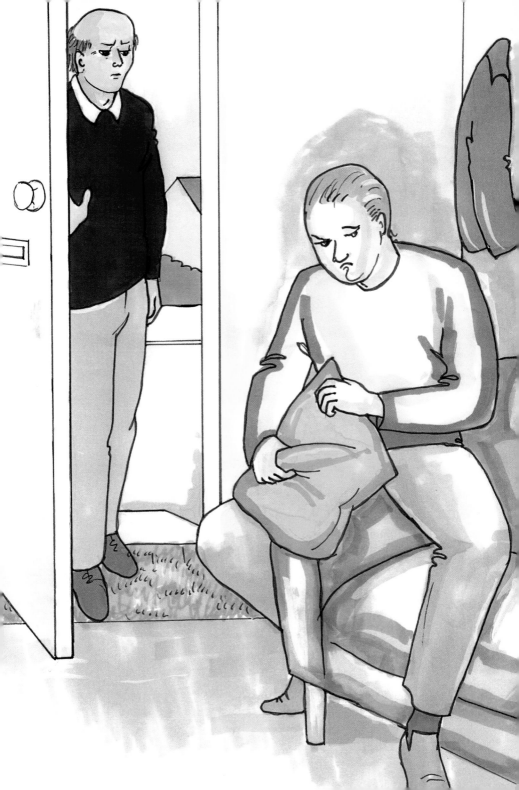

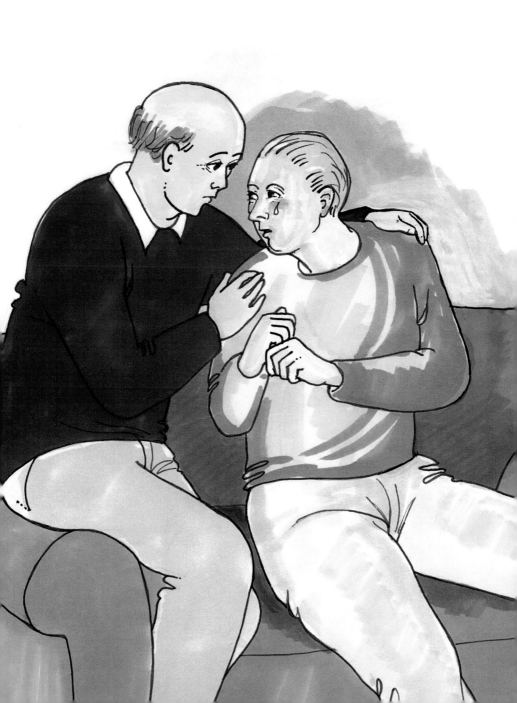

First published 1995 by St George's Mental Health Library.

Second edition published 2015 by Books Beyond Words.

Text & illustrations © Books Beyond Words 2015.

ISBN 978-1-78458-039-1

British Library Cataloguing-in-Publication Data
A catalogue record for this book is available from the British Library.

Printed by Book Printing UK, Peterborough.

Books Beyond Words is a Community Interest Company registered in England and Wales (7557861).

St George's Hospital Charity is a registered charity (no. 241527).

Contents

Storyline

The following words are provided for readers and supporters who want some ideas about one possible story. Most readers make their own story up from the pictures.

1. Neil walks in the park.

2. Neil is alone.

3. He sees a woman. She is alone, too.

4. Neil wants to hug the woman. The woman is cross and frightened. "Go away," she says.

5. The woman runs away. She shouts, "Don't touch strangers!"

6. Neil walks on. Some children play football. He likes football.

7. Neil tries to play with the children.

8. The children shout names at him. They run away. They don't understand.

9. Neil walks on. He sees a couple kissing. He feels warm inside. "Me too!" he thinks.

10. Neil tries to hug them. The man and woman look startled.

11. The couple shout rude things at Neil. They walk away. Neil doesn't understand.

12. Neil walks on. He feels upset and lonely.

13. Neil goes home. He tries not to cry. He thinks, "Nobody likes me."

14. Indoors it is private. Neil punches the door and cries.

15. Neil remembers his friend, Steve, and rings him.

16. "Hello, Steve. This is Neil. Nobody likes me and I'm alone."

17. Someone knocks at the door.

18. Steve comes in. Neil feels embarrassed.

19. Steve says, "What's the matter?" It's hard to explain. Steve waits.

20. Neil tells Steve about the people in the park.

21. Steve comforts Neil. Steve says, "It's OK to hug good friends when we both want to. But it all goes wrong if we touch strangers."

22. Steve says, "Let's go out together. We'll try and do it better."

23. Steve says, "Come and meet my friends. When we meet someone new, we smile and say hello."

24. "We shake hands and say our names. These are my friends Emma and Jake." "Hello, I'm Neil," says Neil.

25. Neil, Steve, Emma and Jake go for a drink. Neil asks Emma about herself. Emma says, "I work in a shop."

26. Emma and Jake dance together. Neil feels jealous.

27. Steve says, "If you want to dance with Emma, you can ask her. She'll say yes if she wants to."

28. Neil says, "Emma, do you want to dance?" Emma says, "Yes."

29. Neil likes dancing with Emma.

30. Neil's new friends walk home with him. "Nice to meet you," they say, and they shake hands with him.

31. "Thank you, Steve," says Neil. "I had a nice time. It was much better – nobody is angry now!"

32. "Goodnight," everyone says. "See you."

33. Neil makes a drink. He thinks about what he knows about touching and hugging.

The importance of friendship

Friendships and relationships are important elements in everyone's life. Without them we can become lonely, and our mental health can suffer.

Making friends can be particularly hard for many people with learning disabilities, who may have fewer social opportunities than other people. They may not have as much choice about their friends, and stick to family and to the people they live with.

Sometimes people who have paid staff think of their staff as friends, but these friendships are often one-sided and can vanish when the workforce changes. People with learning disabilities who do not get any support, on the other hand, may be especially at risk of isolation and depression.

In the story, Neil is lonely and longs for friendship but has little experience of it. When he is shown how to make friends safely, his life begins to change.

Learning the rules

This book deals with a topic that provokes strong reactions. It looks at the unwritten rules of touch between people, using a simple picture story. The story is about Neil, who craves some friendliness or intimacy, but has not yet begun to understand the basics of how to approach people successfully. He is making lots of mistakes, and is confused by other people's horrified reactions.

Neil might have got to adulthood without understanding the rules of consenting touch for a number of reasons. He might have a learning disability, or another condition such as autism, and find social interaction difficult to understand. He might have been brought up in an institutional setting and not experienced normal loving touch, perhaps in a hospital or residential home. He might have been abused as a child, and learned the wrong set of rules.

Perhaps he also missed out on educational opportunities. Many older adults with learning disabilities have missed out on sex and relationships education at school. In the UK all schools now have a responsibility to include pupils with additional needs in an appropriate and accessible way in the PSHE (Personal Social Health and Economic education) curriculum, including sex and relationships education.

The risk to other people

In the story, Neil is not a sex offender. He upsets other people by accident, making naïve mistakes, following his own need for closeness. At first he doesn't pick up on the horrified reactions of the people he approaches; then he is confused and upset by them. He learns very quickly, and the story is a hopeful one.

An adult making these kinds of mistakes might find themselves in all sorts of trouble. Without good support, they could be vulnerable to prosecution and may end up in prison or a secure hospital. The Mental Health Act (2007) includes provisions for people with learning disabilities to be detained, if their disability is associated with abnormally aggressive or seriously irresponsible conduct.

As members of the public, our general judgements of someone who touches us without consent can vary a lot. We weigh up the possible threat to ourselves and our families, and whether we think the person wants to hurt or abuse us, or whether they have just made a mistake and can be diverted easily. There is no one right way to react when you are faced with someone who does not conform to the basic rules of touch; they may indeed pose a real risk to others. Families, carers and professionals are sometimes reluctant to put patterns of behaviour together over the long term, and may accidentally miss a risky pattern by viewing incidents in isolation.

We may need to make snap judgements about people's intentions, and whether they are responsible for the way they behave. We need to think about whether they just don't know the right way to behave, and need an educational intervention, or are behaving in a genuinely risky way. There could be a genuine mistake; they might be concentrating on just a part of someone and not the whole person. Some people have difficulty understanding other people's reactions, for example they may wrongly interpret a scream as a laugh. Specialist therapists can support many people with these types of problems.

While this book can be used as a teaching aid for someone who missed out on being taught, the book can also be used more formally as a reasonable adjustment to support a programme for sex offenders with learning disabilities, to help them discuss and explore the reactions of the victims of crime.

Useful resources in the UK

Services

Community Learning Disability Teams (CLDTs)
These are specialist multidisciplinary health teams that support adults with learning disabilities and their families by assessment of their health needs and a range of clinical interventions. Teams may include therapists and psychologists, who can provide specialist intervention to support communication, activities of daily living, and mental health. CLDTs normally support people who have substantial or critical needs, including those who present a risk to others. Many now have websites and call centres to direct you the right way.

Challenging Behaviour Foundation (CBF)
The CBF offers practical advice to families and professionals to help them understand and support children and adults whose behaviour can challenge. Individual support is available by phone, email or face to face, and there are workshops on positive behaviour support and communication for families and professionals. A range of information on behaviour that challenges, health and caring is also available on the CBF website.
Support service: 0845 602 7885
support@thecbf
www.challengingbehaviour.org.uk

Respond
Respond works with children and adults with learning disabilities who have experienced abuse or trauma,

as well as those who have abused others, through psychotherapy, advocacy, campaigning and other support. Respond also provides training, consultancy and research to combat abuse.
Helpline: 0808 808 0700
www.respond.org.uk

Circles of support
Circles of support provide support to people at risk of isolation or harmful behaviour, helping them to find stability within the community. Circles of support that work with people who show sexually harmful behaviour are also called Circles of Support and Accountability. Circles also help people with learning disabilities who do not show any harmful behaviour, to increase their support networks, friendships and community involvement.

Circles UK supports the development of local Circles of Support and Accountability across England and Wales to reduce the incidence of sex offending. You can find details of local Circles on their website.
www.circles-uk.org.uk/local-projects

Respond provides Circles of Support and Accountability to young people with learning disabilities in London.
020 7380 8259
www.respond.org.uk/what-we-do/cosa/

The **Foundation for People with Learning Disabilities** provide some information about the benefit of circles of support for people with learning disabilities, as well as help to get started.
www.learningdisabilities.org.uk/our-work/family-friends-community/circles-of-support/

Dating services

There are a number of regional dating services specifically for people with learning disabilities. Most offer the opportunity to make new friendships, as well as supported introductions and dates, and events such as speed dating. It is important to check out any service carefully before using it to make sure it is safe and supportive.

London
Stars in the Sky
www.starsinthesky.co.uk

Yorkshire
Luv2MeetU
www.luv2meetu.com

Oxfordshire
Mates 'n' Dates
www.matesndates.org.uk

Scotland
dates-n-mates
www.dates-n-mates.co.uk/

Written materials and online resources

The **BBC** website features a number of videos designed to support PHSE teaching for learners with additional needs. Several focus on appropriate touch and public behaviour.
www.bbc.co.uk/education/topics/zr9dxnb

A 5 is Against the Law. Social Boundaries: Straight Up! An honest guide for teens and young adults, by Kari Dunn Buron. This book is aimed at young people with high-functioning autism who may behave in inappropriate ways because of a lack of social understanding. It aims to help young people judge a situation correctly, increase their social skills, and avoid getting into trouble.

The **Family Planning Association (FPA)** publishes a number of resources focusing on supporting people to express their sexuality safely and effectively.

Sexuality and Learning Disability: A guide to supporting continuing professional development, by Zarine Katrak and Claire Fanstone. This book is aimed at service providers who want to increase their staff's skills. It includes guidance on establishing a sexuality policy, and helpful advice for tackling difficult topics.

Learning Disabilities, Sex and the Law: A practical guide, by Claire Fanstone and Sarah Andrews. This book looks at sexuality in the context of a legal framework. It answers some common questions relating to consent and sexual behaviour.
Both these books can be purchased direct from the FPA.
www.fpa.org.uk/shop/12/product-list

Improving Access to Psychological Therapies (IAPT) *Learning Disabilities Positive Practice Guide* is a guidance document for specialist mental health providers on how to work effectively with people with learning disabilities, and remove barriers to accessing services.
www.iapt.nhs.uk/silo/files/learning-disabilities-positive-practice-guide.pdf

World Health Organisation (WHO) *Better Health, Better Lives. The European Declaration on Children*

and Young People with Intellectual Disabilities and their Families. This document sets out a number of pan-European promises regarding the rights of children with learning disabilities to, for example, health, education and family life, as opposed to an insitutional upbringing. It can be downloaded from the WHO website.
www.euro.who.int/en/health-topics/noncommunicable-diseases/mental-health/publications/2010/european-declaration-on-the-health-of-children-and-young-people-with-intellectual-disabilities-easy-read-version

Legal information
Someone who touches another person without their consent could be charged with common assault or under the Sexual Offences Act (2003).

Information about the Sexual Offences Act and what it covers can be found on the National Archives website.
www.legislation.gov.uk/ukpga/2003/42

The **National Autistic Society** website contains helpful guidance for working with people with autism within the criminal justice system, including getting an assessment under Section 12 of the Mental Health Act (2007).
www.autism.org.uk/working-with/criminal-justice/criminal-justice-system-and-asds.aspx

Related titles in the Books Beyond Words series

Hug Me, Touch Me (2014, 2nd edition) by Sheila Hollins and Terry Roth, illustrated by Beth Webb. Janet wants someone to hug her but always picks the wrong person. This book tells how she learns when she can and can't hug and touch people.

Loving Each Other Safely (2011) by Helen Bailey and Jason Upton, illustrated by Catherine Brighton. Getting close to someone in a relationship is exciting and rewarding. But it's important to stay healthy and safe. This book aims to help young men explore their own sexuality, choose what to do in a steady relationship, and know how to stay healthy.

Falling in Love (1999) by Sheila Hollins, Wendy Perez and Adam Abdelnoor, illustrated by Beth Webb. This love story follows the relationship between Mike and Janet from their first date through to deciding to become engaged to be married.

Feeling Cross and Sorting It Out (2014) by Sheila Hollins and Nick Barratt, illustrated by Beth Webb. Ben doesn't like being rushed, and when Paul won't make time for a chat, Ben gets cross and upset. Jane helps them sort it out. This book will help people communicate about difficult situations and behaviour that can challenge.

George Gets Smart (2001) by Sheila Hollins, Margaret Flynn and Philippa Russell, illustrated by Catherine Brighton. George's life changes when he learns how to keep clean and smart. People no longer avoid him and he enjoys the company of his workmates and friends.

Ron's Feeling Blue (2011, 2nd edition) by Sheila Hollins, Roger Banks and Jenny Curran, illustrated by Beth Webb. Ron is depressed and has no interest in doing things. With the help of his GP and family he begins to feel better.

Sonia's Feeling Sad (2011) by Sheila Hollins and Roger Banks, illustrated by Lisa Kopper. Sonia is feeling so sad that she shuts herself off from her family and friends. She agrees to see a counsellor and gradually begins to feel better.

When Dad Hurts Mum (2014) by Sheila Hollins, Patricia Scotland and Noëlle Blackman, illustrated by Anne-Marie Perks. After her dad is violent towards her mum, Katie is sad and distracted at college. Her teacher supports the family to get the help of an Independent Domestic Violence Advocate. Katie and her mum are kept safe and Katie's dad is court-ordered to join a group to stop his abusive behaviour.

Finding a Safe Place from Abuse (2014) by Sheila Hollins, Patricia Scotland and Noëlle Blackman, illustrated by Anne-Marie Perks. Katie meets David and falls in love. She moves in with him, but the relationship turns difficult and dangerous when David begins to steal money and hurt her physically. Katie quickly gets help through her GP. After a stay in a refuge, Katie begins a new life with a new sense of confidence.

Authors and artist

Sheila Hollins is Emeritus Professor of Psychiatry of Disability at St George's, University of London, and sits in the House of Lords. She is a past President of the Royal College of Psychiatrists and of the BMA, and chairs the BMA's Board of Science. She is founding editor, author and Executive Chair of Books Beyond Words, and a family carer for her son who has a learning disability.

Terry Roth is a practising Clinical Psychologist in Somerset, and Associate Fellow of the British Psychological Society. She specialises in visual aids for simplified psychotherapies, and is a particular Sandplay enthusiast.

Beth Webb is an artist who helped to develop the concept of Books Beyond Words in its early days. She is also the author of fourteen novels for children and young people and is a professional storyteller.

Acknowledgments

With grateful thanks to Nigel Hollins, Madeleine Thomas, Avalon NHS Trust, Somerset Partnership NHS Foundation Trust, service users in Sedgemoor, people at the Enterprise Resource Centre, Bridgwater, and many others whose help and encouragement made this book possible.

Dedication

To Martin

Beyond Words: publications and training

Books Beyond Words will help family carers, support workers and professionals working with people who find pictures easier than words for understanding their world. A list of all Beyond Words publications, including Books Beyond Words titles, and where to buy them, can be found on our website:

www.booksbeyondwords.co.uk

Workshops about using Books Beyond Words are provided regularly in London, or can be arranged in other localities on request. Self-advocates are welcome. For information about forthcoming workshops see our website or contact us:

email: admin@booksbeyondwords.co.uk
tel: 020 8725 5512

Video clips showing our books being read are also on our website and YouTube channel: www.youtube. com/user/booksbeyondwords and on our DVD, *How to Use Books Beyond Words*.

How to read this book

There is no right or wrong way to read this book. Remember it is not necessary to be able to read the words.

1. Some people are not used to reading books. Start at the beginning and read the story in each picture. Encourage the reader to hold the book themselves and to turn the pages at their own pace.

2. Whether you are reading the book with one person or with a group, encourage them to tell the story in their own words. You will discover what each person thinks is happening, what they already know, and how they feel. You may think something different is happening in the pictures yourself, but that doesn't matter. Wait to see if their ideas change as the story develops. Don't challenge the reader(s) or suggest their ideas are wrong.

3. Some pictures may be more difficult to understand. It can help to prompt the people you are supporting, for example:

- Who do you think that is?
- What is happening?
- What is he or she doing now?
- How is he or she feeling?
- Do you feel like that? Has it happened to you/ your friend/ your family?

4. You don't have to read the whole book in one sitting. Allow people enough time to follow the pictures at their own pace.

5. Some people will not be able to follow the story, but they may be able to understand some of the pictures. Stay a little longer with the pictures that interest them.